© I CAN 2011

Contents

Making a Difference	2
Framework for supporting children's speech, language and communication development	5
1 Information	6
2 Knowledge and skills	8
3 Planning	9
4 Adult-child interaction	10
5 Working with parents and families	12
6 Working with other partners	13
7 Measuring outcomes	14
Your next steps in making a difference	18
Appendix – resources	19
Baby/child typical language development	22
Checklist of adult's use of language	24
Checklist of what to consider in the environment	25
The speech, language and communication framework (self-audit tool)	26

Making a Difference

Developing good practice in young children's communication

We know that supporting babies' and young children's speech, language and communication skills makes a big difference in their lives: "Effective oral language skills are the building blocks on which subsequent literacy and numeracy development is based. Without solid foundations in language and communication skills, children run the risk of school failure, low self esteem and poor social skills."[1]

So, knowing this, how can we make it happen?

This tool is aimed at anyone providing a service to children under five and their families – whether you are a childminder, manage a Children's Centre or provide group sessions in Children's Centres, libraries or in your local community hall. It will help to develop good practice in supporting children's speech, language and communication (SLC) skills.

Speech, language and communication development and its impact on other areas of learning

In case you are not already convinced, recent evidence signposting the importance of good SLC is widely available[2,3]. The development of these skills has now been embraced into government policy[4].

The 2011 Tickell review of the Early Years Foundation Stage recommended that communication is seen as one of the three essential foundations for life, learning and success[5].

The value of communication in building relationships, in finding out about how things work, in understanding rules and expectations and in getting on in life is now agreed. Without good communication skills, children struggle with learning but also with their emotional development[6].

Moreover, children's language skills, as young as two years of age, are a predictor of their performance on entry to primary school[7].

We can help with school readiness - what we do now makes a difference both now and later.

---

[1] Hartshorne, M (2006) *The Cost to the Nation of Children's Poor Communication*, I CAN Talk Series, Issue 2
[2] Ibid
[3] Freeman, K and Hartshorne, M (2009) *Speech, Language and Communication Needs in the Early Years*, I CAN Talk series, Issue 7
[4] DfE (2011) Tender Specification Early Years Language Development Training Programme
[5] Tickell, Dame C (2011)The Early Years: Foundations for life, health and learning: *An Independent Report on the Early Years Foundation Stage to Her Majesty's Government*
[6] Lees and Unwin (1997) *Children with Language Disorders*. Whurr Publications
[7] Roulstone, S, Law, J, Rush, R, Clegg, J and Peters, T (2011) *Investigating the role of language in children's early educational outcomes* University of the West of England, Bristol

Adults making a difference

As well as parents having a key role to play at home, the communication environment in the early years has been found to be crucial in ensuring school readiness and lowering the risk of poor attainment[8].

Early years settings, their staff and other adults providing services to children are very important in supporting early communication development. It seems that what happens in the setting is more important in supporting communication development than the type of setting[9].

The book *Understanding Communication Development*[10] (available from I CAN) explains more about how speech, language and communication skills develop and your role in supporting them.

We know what helps

As well as the research that shows that early support for SLC skills is essential, we also know the impact of key aspects of support. These include:

- **A focus on communication in the early years**[11]
- **The need for a skilled and confident workforce**[12]
- **Focused early intervention**[13]
- **Integrated approaches**[14] with different organisations and staff working closely together
- **Working closely with parents**[15]

All of these are described later in this document. So if you want to make sure that you're doing your best to support children's communication development, consider all the aspects carefully.

Even if you are considering all of the above, how do you know what you are doing works?

The key to finding out how much you're making a difference is to measure the difference made by what you do. This can also be used to convince other people of your successes (useful for those who are selling services to commissioners, children's centres or local authorities).

Once you know whether you are making a difference, you can also adjust what you're doing, to make that difference even bigger.

---

[8] Hart, B. and Risley, RR (1995) *Meaningful Differences in the Everyday Experience of Young American Children*. Baltimore: Paul Brookes
[9] Sylva, K, Melhuish, EC, Sammons, P, Siraj-Blatchford, I and Taggart, B (2004),*The Effective Provision of Pre-School Education (EPPE) Project: Technical Paper 12 - The Final Report: Effective Pre-School Education*. London: DfES. Institute of Education, University of London.
[10] I CAN (2011) *Understanding Communication Development*
[11] Tickell, Dame C. (2011) *The Early Years: Foundations for life, health and learning: An Independent Report on the Early Years Foundation Stage to Her Majesty's Government*
[12] Ofsted (2006) *Inclusion: Does it really matter where pupils are taught?*
[13] Hartshorne, M (2006) *The Cost to the Nation of Children's Poor Communication*, I CAN Talk Series, Issue 2
[14] Law, J, Lindsay, G, Peacey, N, Gascoigne, M, Soloff, N, Radford, J and Brand, S (2000) *Provision for children with speech and language needs in England and Wales*, DfEE
[15] Evangelou, M, Sylv, K, Edward, A and Smith, T (2008) *The Birth to school study: A longitudinal evaluation of the Peers Early Education Project (PEEP)* Sure Start

Putting it into practice

Making a Difference to children's SLC development means thinking about how to do this throughout the day. Think about:

- **Opportunities you offer the children**
- **Information that you give to parents**
- **Changes that you will make to your setting or group**

We have pulled the key considerations into a framework for supporting children's SLC development.

You can work through the framework a bit at a time or divide it up so that individual members of staff look at particular areas. If you are looking at particular areas, choose the one most appropriate for you. You do not have to work through this framework in order, the numbers used are for ease of reference.

You can get outside help to assist you in the process (see 'next steps' section at the end of the book).

How you decide to use the framework depends very much on the nature of your work with young children, the number of staff you work with and the length of time you want to take. However, we do know that all of these aspects will help you to make a difference to children's communication development.

Framework for supporting children's speech, language and communication development

The framework for supporting children's SLC development consists of seven areas. You will need to consider each of these areas to make the biggest difference.

Framework areas:

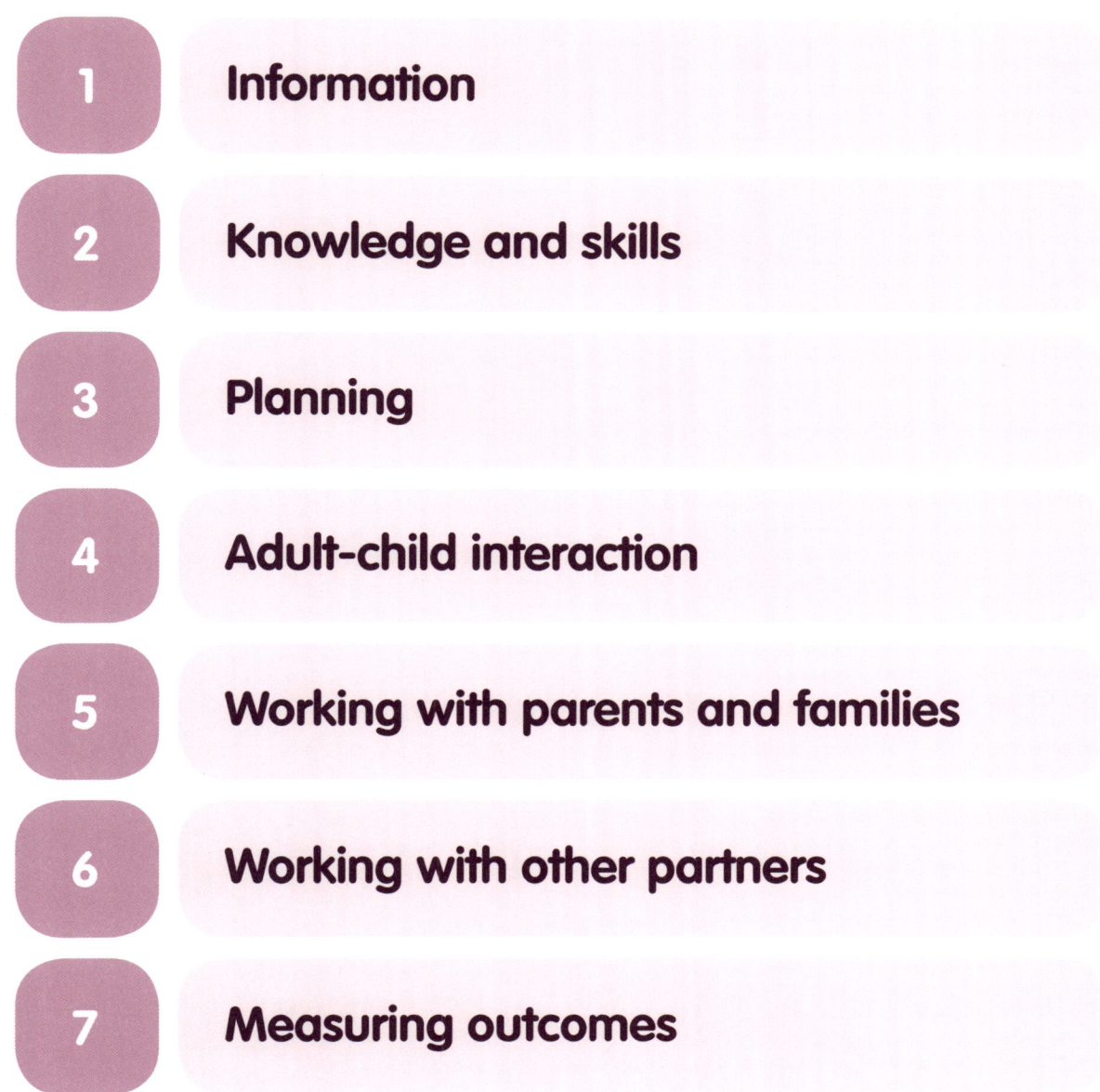

1. Information
2. Knowledge and skills
3. Planning
4. Adult-child interaction
5. Working with parents and families
6. Working with other partners
7. Measuring outcomes

We will take each one of these areas in turn and explore what is meant, so that you can think about how it applies to your service or session/s.

1 Information

Type of information needed

The Bercow Review into speech, language and communication needs[16] identified that parents don't have enough information about what to expect from children's SLC development and any concerns that they have.

Information is needed for both staff and parents. It is essential that people who spend time with young children have information on:

- **The importance of SLC development**
- **How to support SLC development**
- **What to expect at different ages**
- **What to do if you're worried**

Information for parents can be in a variety of forms (spoken or written, words or pictures). It needs to be consistent so that people don't get mixed messages.

Think about how information can be made available to people with low literacy levels or for whom English is an additional language. (Remember that not everyone who can speak a particular language knows how to read that same language).

Additional information is needed for practitioners:

- **Practitioners need information on how to evaluate the outcomes of their work to support children's SLC development (see the section on 'Measuring outcomes').**
- **Staff also need guidelines and processes for raising concerns about a child's SLC development and referring to professional support as appropriate, with parent/s' consent. You may have a SLC support policy which provides this information, or you could develop one**.

[16] Bercow (2008) *Bercow Review of Services for Children and Young People (0-19) with Speech, Language and Communication Needs.* Department for Schools, Children and Families

How information can be provided

There are lots of posters, booklets, books and DVDs that are suitable for both parents and practitioners. Details of some of these are found in the 'Resources' section in the appendix (page19), at the back of this guide. There is also information on stages of SLC development here.

You need to decide how you are going to make this information available, some suggestions are:

- **Staff/parent noticeboards.**

- **Distribute in staff/parent welcome packs.**

- **Open days or parents' evenings.**

- **Newsletters.**

- **Make visible to parents when they pick their children up, e.g. leaflet stand.**

- **When discussing children's progress with parents.**

- **Campaigns such as 'Ditch the dummy', or 'Turn off the telly'.**

- **A summary poster (or similar) could be considered. This could include details of top tips to support SLC development as well as how outcomes are measured in your setting. It could also include the process for identifying children of concern.**

- **Create small 'credit card' sized cards with information summaries to share with families.**

Tip

It is worth checking what people think of the information that you have made available, what else they want to know and whether they making use of it?

Knowledge and skills

We know that a skilled and confident workforce is key to supporting SLC development.
Consider how you and any other staff are supported to:

- **Develop and apply knowledge of typical SLC development from birth to five years.**
- **Understand that language skills underpin all learning, as well as social, emotional and behavioural aspects of development.**
- **Work with children for whom English is an additional language.**
- **Recognise that some children do not follow the typical pattern of SLC development[17] and this might indicate that they have SLC needs (SLCN).**
- **Recognise the importance of professional / personal development in having a positive impact on the communication development of all children.**
- **Access training and development opportunities around SLC on an annual basis. This could take a variety of formats, drop-in speakers or sessions to parent groups, a leaflet or flyer with 'top tips', induction information, etc. (see the Resources section in the appendix for materials that may help you).**
- **Have time to reflect on practice around SLC and discuss strategies with colleagues.
(A checklist of SLC strategies is provided in the appendix).**

Staff can monitor progress with their development of knowledge and skills through the Speech, Language and Communication Framework (SLCF).

Further information about staff skills and the SLCF is available in the appendix (page 26) or on
www.communicationhelppoint.org.uk

Details of qualifications such as the Children's and Young People's Level 3 Workforce Diploma or the level 3 certificate in speech, language and communication can be found on the Communication Trust website:
www.thecommunicationtrust.org.uk

[17] More information about the ages and stages of SLC development can be found in the appendix and is also available on www.talkingpoint.org.uk

3 Planning

"He who fails to plan is planning to fail". Winston Churchill's words can refer, in this case, to the importance of planning support for SLC development.

All staff have a responsibility to plan their work with children. When working to make a difference, think about how you and any other staff are supported to:

- **Have the time to plan and review SLC focused activities.**
- **Think about the adult role in the activity with children.**
- **Think about how and when you can reflect on activities and how this reflection changes what happens in the future.**
- **Develop activities and actions based on feedback from parent consultations and consultation with children, their families and other agencies.**
- **Arrange training and development opportunities.**
- **Work in a systematic way to support SLC development, often using approaches which are seen (through research articles or reports) to have positive outcomes.**
- **Have clear and explicit objectives (targets) and a detailed activity plan to focus on SLC as part of a service, session or activity.**
- **Have access to and share with parents, information about SLC development, ages and stages, top tips and what to do if they are worried.**
- **Create settings or groups which parents feel support their child's SLC development.**
- **Create language supportive outdoor and indoor environments which promote talking between (or among) children, as well as between children and adults.**

Use the checklist (page 25) about what to consider in the environment to help you plan more effectively.

Making a Difference © I CAN 2011

 # Adult - child interaction

Skilled staff understand the importance of the interaction between themselves and the children they work with. Think about how you're going to make sure that this happens in your setting or group.

The information below gives an idea of how adults need to be interacting with the children they are working with.

With children from birth – 3 years, positive interaction includes:

- **Responding to communicative attempts from babies, promoting early communicative interaction.** For example, adults making sure they are in close proximity with the baby, using eye contact, positive facial expression and simple language to respond and interact.

- **Identifying opportunities when relationships and interactions can be used to promote SLC.** For example, how time spent on physical care (changing nappies, washing, dressing etc) is used as an opportunity for the child to experience interaction (rather than the adult focusing on task completion); how books are used to encourage understanding of words and attention; or how quiet areas are created to encourage language development.

- **Making effective observations of individual children and using these to interpret the child's wants, needs and feelings. Then naming the interpretation and letting the child know at an appropriate language level.** For example, if a baby points to their cup, the adult may interpret that they want a drink. This can be named by saying, 'Juice?' If the baby is smiling or crying, the adult can interpret this by saying 'You're happy/ sad/angry/tired'. If the child is laughing, the adult can say, 'Is that funny?'

- **Understanding and knowing how to use language at an appropriate level with the child.** For example, accepting baby language such as 'ta', 'doggy' and then saying the adult version in response, e.g. 'Yes, it's a dog'. Or adding one word onto the length of sentence used by the child e.g. Child says, 'Big bear' and the adult says 'Yes, big cuddly bear'.

With all children, positive interaction includes:

Using a range of strategies to support children's SLC development, for example:

- Simple, repetitive language during everyday activities.
- Gaining children's attention before giving instructions.
- Talking at an appropriate rate, using short sentences.
- Adapting language to the level of the child's.
- Demonstrating the correct sentence when a child's incorrect utterance is heard. So, if a child says, 'I runned', the adult can say, 'Oh, you ran, did you?'
- Extending the child's utterances – if they say, '*bus*', respond saying '*big bus*'.
- Encouraging the children to ask questions.
- Using vocabulary the children can understand in everyday instructions.
- Giving children time to process information and respond.
- Giving a running commentary on the child's activity, rather than asking questions most of the time.
- Using natural gestures and facial expressions to support language.
- Listening to the children and responding to what they say, rather than directing their communication with lots of questions.
- Allowing plenty of time for children to process what they have heard and prepare a response, before they talk back.

For a useful checklist to monitor adult's use of language and essential information about typical language development stages in babies and young children, see page 24.

 # Working with Parents/families

Parenting is identified as a much stronger predictor of children's progress than any childcare experience[18]. Those working with young children have a responsibility to provide information to parents about their children and what is happening in the activity/session. However, they can also support parents by providing information about SLC development and what can be done to reinforce it (see 'Information' section).

Also think about:

- **Showing parents, through the way that you talk with young children, how to support children's SLC development.**
- **Letting parents know about what other services are available to support their needs - specifically targeting individuals or families who traditionally have found it difficult to access the information, ie. families where English is not spoken at home, fathers and other male care givers and socially disadvantaged families.**
- **Meeting the ethnic, cultural and linguistic backgrounds of families when promoting children's SLC development.** For example, using positive behaviours towards children using different languages and letting parents know to use, value and develop their home language.
- **Valuing the role and contribution of families, peers and friends to a child's communication development.**
- **Highlighting to families how they can contact Speech and Language Therapy departments if they have concerns about their child's communication development.** (Many Speech and Language Therapy departments run an 'open referral system', so parents can ask for an assessment themselves, if they are worried).
- **Supporting families through evidence-based support programmes, which show how the provision will make a difference to children's outcomes.** For example, offering parenting programmes using a structured approach with a proven track record in improving parenting skills and promoting positive parenting.
- **Exploring with parents issues around communication through offering specific sessions,** e.g. *Exploring Communication Development: A resource for working with parents*[19].

In any aspect of work with young children, think about how parents let you know what they like / don't like, or want or feel. How can parents let you know what they think about what you are doing, or give you ideas about what they would like? Is it worth having a parent on your management group if you have one?

---

[18] Belsky, J, Lowe Vandell, D, Burchinal, M, Clarke-Stewart, K.A, McCartney, K, Tresch Owenm M (2007) *Are there long term effects of childcare?* Child Development Vol. 78, Number 2, pp 681-701 The NICHD Early Childcare Research Network
[19] I CAN (2011) *Exploring Communication Development*

6 Working with other Partners

At the start of this guide, we noted that services successfully supporting SLC development are often those where organisations and individuals work closely with each other. Important aspects of partnership working include:

- **Leaders and managers liaising appropriately with local groups and agencies to co-ordinate approaches to provision for SLC development.** Find out what is happening locally and see how what you offer could fit together with this.
- **Using commissioning arrangements to develop effective multi-agency work (data sharing agreements may need to be discussed).**
- **Different practitioners and organisations having time together.** This can help with planning for and reflecting on approaches that support children's SLC and identify children with SLCN. Are there network or sector meetings that you could join? Could you arrange some joint training? Or, could you arrange for a visit or 'staff swap' for a session with another practitioner or group?
- **Working with other people or organisations to provide parents and staff with the information they need to effectively support children's SLC development or needs (See section on 'Information').**
- **Considering how to involve parents in discussion and action planning.**
- **Ensuring parents are involved particularly if there are concerns about their child's SLC development.**
- **Understanding and working with the policies of other, related services.** For example, knowing how to access support from speech and language therapists or how to feed into assessments carried out by health practitioners (in England, the Healthy Child Review).

7 Measuring outcomes

How do you know you are making a difference?

As we have seen, you are well placed to support children's SLC skills. A range of activities and approaches can be used for this. Specific activities can include rhyme time, baby signing, chatter groups, parent support sessions, etc.

However, it is important to be clear about whether the activities we provide, or the approaches we use, actually do make a difference to the children or parents we support.

Setting the targets

When setting up activities or sessions, think about what the aim is, what skill is being supported and what difference will the activity make to the child and / or their family. This is the first step in measuring outcomes – only if you know what you are aiming for, will you be able to check whether your target has been achieved.

Useful things to think about are:

- **The type of activity: What is the activity, who is it aimed at – children or adults, targeted or universal?**
- **The intended outcomes of the activity: What do you want to achieve?** For example, parents are better informed about children's SLC development; or children talk more at the end of a set of sessions than they did at the beginning of the set; or carers use more commenting language with their children and less directive language.
- **How you can collect the information / data about what has changed?** You could use questionnaires, interviews, assessment, or observations. Think about the evidence you need to show whether or not you have made the difference you were hoping for.
- **When you collect this information make sure you have a 'baseline'. This is a measure taken before or at the beginning of your activity and it provides something to compare the end result to.**
- **How robust is the measurement? Are you sure it really measures what you think it does?**
  For example, do changes in eye contact reflect changes the adult is making to how they interact with the child or how interested the child is in the activity the adult is doing?

How to measure outcomes

There are many different types of measurement that can be taken These will obviously be different according to the activity involved. Examples are:

- **Measures of parent/carers' confidence in how to help children's SLC development.**
- **Measures of staff and parents' communication with the children, using a before and after rating scale.** For example, how many times does the parent wait for the child to start conversations rather than asking the child a question? Compare before and after the parent support was offered. (You can also use observation with a checklist or video observation).
- **Measures of staff competencies around SLC.** For example, staff using the online self-audit tool Speech, Language and Communication Framework[20] to see the level of their skills and knowledge (**www.communicationhelppoint.org.uk**).
- **Measures of children's communication behaviours.** For example assessments, observations, checklists or profiles that have been carried out before the activity took place, compared with the same assessment, observation, checklist or profile after it. Remember to take into account the child's change in age over the period of the activity. Is the change more than would be expected just from a change in age?

[20] The Communication Trust *Speech, Language and Communication Framework* www.thecommunicationtrust.org.uk

Examples of activities and types of outcome measure that could be used.

We have listed here possible activities and examples of targets which you might use as outcome measures or evidence of change.

Activity	Outcome measure
Educational outcomes for children	Evidence could be available through: OFSTED evaluation HMIe inspections (Scotland) Baseline measures of Communication Language and Literacy Tracking forms such as EYFS / ECaT[21] Curriculum planning frameworks (CfE Scotland)
Early Years Language groups, such as:	
Baby signing	Evidence of improved interaction between parent and child – using before and after observations.
Chatter groups or sound groups	Evidence that children's communication behaviour is improved – before and after checklists. Parents report that they are more confident in talking to their children – using questionnaires to parents, or parental reports or interviews where parents are asked to rate the group.
Stay & Play session	Communication-supportive environment has been set up – evidence could be through an independent observation of the environment using a checklist such as the one in the appendix, or observations of change in children's communication over time. Other evidence might be parents reporting that they are confident in playing with and talking to their children. You could also investigate if Stay & Play staff are confident to support SLC development, as a result of training. To find this out, use questionnaires, or staff self-rating scales or the speech, language and communication framework described in the appendix.
Fathers' book group	Evidence could be the number of fathers who have joined a library, or fathers reporting that they read with children regularly. Another type of evidence might be the continued attendance at the group.

[21] Every Child a Talker – DCSF programme run between 2008 and 2011

Activity	Outcome measure
Early Years Language groups, such as:	
Informal drop-in sessions	The target might be that 'planning shows evidence of thinking about good practice in SLC. Parents have access to information on SLC. Staff can identify children as needing further support with SLC.' Evidence could be gathered through using the planning documents, referrals to speech and language therapy, the number of parents who have taken information on SLC or who know about issues in this area.
Special Educational Needs / Additional Support for Learning groups	Try a staff or parent questionnaire – before and after the group sessions.
Parent groups – visiting speakers, etc	A questionnaire could be used or an interview to find whether parents report that they are confident regarding SLC development
2-year-old support	The target might be 'to increase identification and referral of children with significant SLC needs'. Evidence can be gathered through the number of children referred appropriately to speech and language therapy. If the target was 'Parents are confident in meeting the communication needs of their children', evidence could be gathered to see whether parents' communication behaviours with children are good. You could use an observation checklist or video observation.
Staff training such as Elklan[22], Hanen[23]	The target of 'developing good knowledge and understanding of SLC development'. Evidence could be gathered through observing practice, or through gathering information on staff's continuing professional development (CPD). 'Good identification and referral' could be another target outcome, as could 'Change in environment such as use of visual systems' or 'sharing information with parents' or 'signposting to agencies'.

[22] Elkan - **www.elkan.co.uk**
[23] Hanen - **www.hanen.org**

Your next steps in making a difference

Following this framework and checking that you are making a difference to children's SLC development means that you have already made a promising start.

If you want to find out more, develop your skills further or get independent support or a validation of your good practice, there are opportunities to do all of these:

- **Find out more** – the resources section in the appendix gives plenty of information about how to find out more about children's SLC development and needs. It is also important to keep up to date with changes in policy or practice that might affect your work in this area and to find out information about what other people are doing that works. Try signing up to one of the regular newsletters available focusing on SLC development.

- There are a large variety of **training courses** to support your knowledge and skills development. These include courses focused on working with parents, on developing activities aimed at particular aspects of SLC development or working in specialist teams. Some of the courses lead to recognised qualifications. More information on courses and qualifications can be found through I CAN (**www.ican.org.uk** or telephone **0845 225 4071**) or The Communication Trust (**www.thecommunicationtrust.org.uk**).

- **I CAN Validation of Good Practice:** Settings, childminders, services or groups might wish for some support in *Making a Difference*. Support includes developing the framework described in this document and looking to see if you are making a difference to children's SLC development.

To find out more details on support and validation, go to **www.ican.org.uk** or phone **0845 225 4071.**

Appendix - resources

For parents and practitioners:

Talking Point (www.talkingpoint.org.uk) is designed for parents and people who work with children. This one-stop information portal contains everything you need to know about supporting children's speech and language development. *Talking Point* helps you to identify if a child is having difficulties or falling behind. If they are struggling, then it tells you what to do. The site contains valuable resources which can be downloaded and used to support children, and links to lots of other places that can help.
It also features an interactive Progress Checker tool to check the development of children's language development at: **http://www.talkingpoint.org.uk/Parent/Directory/Progress-Checker.aspx**

Small Talk – Available from The Communication Trust (**www.communicationtrust.org.uk**). This booklet provides information about what helps children aged 0-5 learn to talk and listen, whether they are on the right track and what to do if the parents have concerns about their child.

I CAN Top techniques poster – Available to download from the I CAN book shop, this poster provides top tips for early years practitioners to develop children's communication.

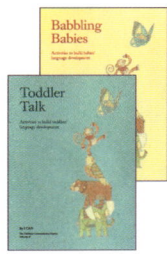

Babbling Babies and Toddler Talk – Packed with 30 inspiring, beautifully illustrated activities for parents and adults to play and develop a baby's communication skills, these cards provide clear, imaginative ways to interact with under-threes. Developed by expert practitioners, each activity has an idea for babies from birth to 6 months, 6 – 12 months and 12 – 18 months and for toddlers from 18 months to 3 years old. Available in a paperback and a hardback edition.

Talk to your Baby – Part of the National Literacy Trust, this organisation provides lots of information and updates on research to support communication development with children under-three **www.literacytrust.org.uk/talk_to_your_baby**

I CAN Communicate – A subscriber-based monthly e-newsletter providing tips, resources and information on SLCN as well as conferences, training, policy and more.
Subscribe at: **www.ican.org.uk/register**

For parents:

Chatter Matters DVD – This DVD contains a fascinating programme presented by Dr Tanya Byron (*House of Tiny Tearaways, Little Angels*) offering dozens of brilliant ideas to help you develop your child's speaking and listening skills throughout their preschool years. Includes a series of colourful mini-posters that enable you to check the progress of your child's communication development.

First Words poster – An A3 fold-up poster showing each year from 0 – 5. Three characteristics of developing communication are listed highlighting how to follow the progress of children's speech, language and communication development. Plus top tips and signposting for help.

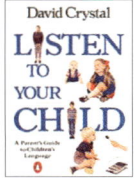
Listen To Your Child – By David Crystal: Penguin Health Books 1986.

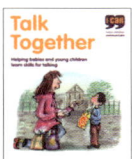
Talk Together – A simple 8-page illustrated booklet which explains to parents the importance of language and milestones to look for.

For practitioners:

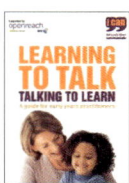
Learning to Talk – A self-study DVD resource for developing young children's slc. presented by Dr Tanya Byron (*House of Tiny Tearaways and Little Angels*). It also offers information on what to do if there are concerns about a child's speech, language and communication development.

Ages and stages of Speech, Language and Communication Development – This poster contains information about children's speech and language development up to five years old.

GP/Health Visitors' checklist – A durable, A5 cribsheet, this checklist contains key information about speech, language and communication development from birth to five years. It can be used when faced with concerned parents, or to cross-reference questions raised during appointments.

From Birth to Five Years: Children's Developmental Progress – By Mary D. Sheridan, Ajay Sharma, and Helen Cockerill: 3rd Ed. Routledge 2007.

From I CAN:

Information on Learning to Talk, Ages and Stages, GP/HV checklist, UCD, ECD, Early Talk Training and Early Talk 0-3 training available at **www.ican.org.uk**

Understanding Communication Toolkit – An I CAN Toolkit which gives early years practitioners and childminders a range of resources to understand, enable and reinforce good practice in supporting children's speech, language and communication (SLC).

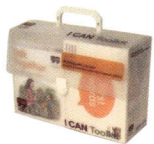

Exploring Communication Development Toolkit – An I CAN Toolkit which gives early years practitioners a range of resources to explore with parents how to support their child's speech, language and communication.

From The Communication Trust:

Universally Speaking – This booklet gives advice and guidance on how to encourage communication in children aged birth to five, explains what children will likely be doing at a given age and gives top tips for what you can do as a practitioner and in a setting. It is available from The Communication Trust **www.thecommunicationtrust.org.uk**

Speech Language and Communication Framework (SLCF):
The SLCF lists all the skills and knowledge that everyone working with children needs to know to support the communication development of all children and those with SLCN. Practitioners who work with children can complete the SLCF online to evaluate their skills and knowledge of communication development. Visit: **http://www.communicationhelppoint.org.uk**

Other useful books and resources:

Every Child a Talker (ECaT) – The first instalment includes an audit tool for evaluating current language provision and identifying priorities for improvement.

Communication Language and Literacy (CLLD) – An audit originally developed by National Strategies now available at:
www.clg.coventry.gov.uk/downloads/file/1036/clld_nursery_audit

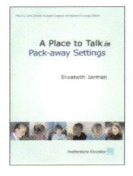

A Place to Talk – A series of publications packed with images of spaces to encourage children to talk. Available in different settings, by Elizabeth Jarman.
Visit: **www.elizabethjarmantraining.co.uk**

Baby / child typical language development

Each language has its own development milestones. Where descriptions of sounds, words and sentences are used below, these apply to learners of English as a first language.

(When working with children for whom English is not their first language, account should be taken of what individual children are doing in their first language. Use an interpreter to find out how things are going.)

6 Months

- Vocalisation with intonation
- Babbles short sequence of sound, e.g. 'da-da, da-da'
- Laughs, chuckles, squeals
- Cries to show distress
- Responds to human voices without visual cues by turning his head and eyes
- Begins to enjoy music and rhymes

12 Months

- Responds to own name
- Recognises some single words in context
- Uses one or more words with meaning (this may be unintelligible to unfamiliar listeners or a fragment of a word)
- Understands simple instructions such as 'come here' or 'clap hands', especially if vocal or physical cues are given
- Gestures to ask for things
- Enjoys games like 'peek-a-boo'

18 Months

- Has vocabulary of approximately 20-50 words
- Vocabulary made up chiefly of nouns
- Is able to follow simple commands, 'Pass me the ball'; 'Bring your shoes'

Download a Stages of Development poster at www.ican.org.uk/bookshop

24 Months

- Is able to understand at least two prepositions, ie 'in', 'on' or 'under'
- Starts using negative – 'There no cat'
- Using plurals
- Starts combining words
- Vocabulary of approximately 50 plus words
- Responds to such commands as 'Show me your eyes (nose, mouth, hair)'

36 Months

- Can engage in simple conversations
- Uses pronouns: 'you', 'me' correctly
- Knows at least three prepositions, usually: 'in', 'on', 'under'
- Knows main parts of body and should be able to indicate these
- Is able to easily understand sentences with three key words, 'Let's find the white car'
- Has approximately 900 to 1000 words
- Verbs begin to develop
- Understands most simple questions dealing with their environment and activities

48 Months

- Asks lots of questions
- Knows names of familiar animals
- Can use at least four prepositions or can demonstrate understanding of their meaning when given commands
- Names common objects in picture books or magazines
- Can usually repeat words of four syllables
- Demonstrates understanding of 'over' and 'under'
- Can tell long stories and sequence events
- Can use language to share, turn-take, argue, collaborate
- Readily follows simple commands
- Beginning to describe how others feel
- Speech should be understood by strangers

Checklist of adult's use of language

Do you:

☐ Say the child's name to get their attention?

☐ Make appropriate eye contact?

☐ Use a variety of tones of voice?

☐ Use natural gesture to support spoken language?

☐ Keep language simple?

☐ Give one instruction at a time?

☐ Check understanding?

☐ Slow down?

☐ Re-phrase information – avoid complex language, e.g. 'The teddy wants to be washed by Jim?'

☐ Think about word order – say things in the order they need to happen?

☐ Comment on what is happening?

☐ Extend children's level of language – 'Doggie.' 'Oh yes, big doggie?'

☐ Repeat language?

☐ Wait for the child to process information and respond?

☐ Make sure that if parents have requested that the child uses a dummy, this is only available at sleeptimes and is removed once the child has woken up?

Checklist of what to consider in the environment:

- [ ] How easy is it for the child to see you and other children when speaking and when listening?
- [ ] Do you have few visual distractions near areas where you are trying to focus on speaking and listening skills?
- [ ] What is the lighting like? Have you considered sunlight from windows and how it moves around the room? (This will have an impact on how easy it is for children to see your face)
- [ ] Which are the noisiest / quietest areas of your setting, or times of day that are noisier or quieter than others? What can you do about these?
- [ ] How easy is it for the child to get your attention?
- [ ] Does the child need to ask you for specific resources?
- [ ] Is the child able to tell you when something is not working – e.g. a piece missing from a jigsaw?
- [ ] What visual reminders do you have (at the child's eye level) about good speaking and listening skills? (for older children)
- [ ] Is there constant noise in the setting that could be turned off eg radio / music / TV?

The speech, language and communication framework (self audit-tool) www.communicationhelppoint.org.uk

Strand A / Typical Speech, Language and Communication Development and Use

	Competence	Example of indicator of competence
	The practitioner will	Consider if you can
Universal A1	You will be aware of what the terms 'speech', 'language' and 'communication' mean and how they are used to describe typical development.	Describe the terms 'speech', 'language' and 'communication'.
Universal A2	You will be aware that speech and language development should follow a typical pattern.	Identify where you can find information on typical speech, language and communication development.
Universal A3	You will be aware that most children and young people who learn English as an additional language follow a typical pattern of development.	Identify where you can find relevant information on English as an additional language.
Universal A4	You will be aware that some children and young people do not follow the typical pattern of speech and language development and that this might mean that they have speech, language and communication needs (SLCN).	Identify where you can find information which highlights that some children do not follow the typical pattern of speech and language development and that this might mean that they have SLCN.
Universal A5	You will be aware that communication includes social skills.	Give an example of how social skills link to communication.
Universal A6	You will be aware that language is about understanding as well as talking.	Give an example that shows a child's or young person's understanding of language.
Universal A7	You will be aware that communication skills are developed through interacting with other people.	Give an example of where a child's interactions with another person show their communication skills developing.
Universal A8	You will be aware that the home environment and other settings affect children's and young people's development and use of language.	Give an example of things which happen in the home which might affect language development.
Universal A9	You will be aware that language skills are the basis for all learning.	Give an example of where language is important in learning a new skill.

Strand B / Identifying and assessing SLCN

	Competence	Example of indicator of competence
	The practitioner will:	Consider if you can:
Universal B1	You will be aware that children and young people may have difficulties with speech, language or communication.	Give an example of a difficulty children or young people may have with speech, language or communication.
Universal B2	You will be aware of how common SLCN are among the general population.	Describe how many children and young people in the UK have SLCN.
Universal B3	You will be aware of what to look for to help identify children and young people in your workplace who may have SLCN.	Give an example of what you might see when a child or young person has difficulty with speech, language or communication in your workplace.
Universal B4	You will be aware that it is also important to identify the effects of a child's or young person's environment on their speech, language and communication development. This includes how adults use language in the environment.	Explain how a situation or the language an adult uses may affect a child's or young person's speech, language and communication development.
Universal B5	You will be aware of some of the ways in which difficulties with speech, language and communication can affect a child or young person you work with.	Explain one way in which a difficulty with speech, language or communication could affect a child or young person in your workplace.
Universal B6	You will be aware that there is a range of reasons for a child or young person to have SLCN.	List some relevant reasons why a child or young person may have SLCN.
Universal B7	You will be aware of how common it is for children and young people who speak English as an additional language to have SLCN.	Explain that it is as common for children and young people who have English as an additional language to have SLCN as those who do not.
Universal B8	You will be aware of how to raise concerns about the speech, language and communication development of children and young people where you work.	Describe how you would raise concerns about the speech, language and communication development of children and young people where you work.

Strand C / Positive Practice

	Competence	Example of indicator of competence
	The practitioner will:	Consider if you can:
Universal C1	You will be aware of and use positive ways to communicate with children and young people where you work.	Describe how you use positive ways to communicate with children and young people where you work.
Universal C2	You will be aware of some of the features that promote a positive communication environment.	List some of the features of your workplace that promote positive communication, including examples of how adult language is used.
Universal C3	You will be aware of some of the positive strategies to support the speech, language and communication development of children and young people you work with.	Describe some particular strategies you can use to support the speech, language and communication development of the children and young people you work with.
Universal C4	You will be aware of the role of communication in getting the views of children and young people.	List ways of getting the views of children and young people in your workplace, highlighting the role of communication.
Universal C5	You will be aware of the existing systems where you work for collecting appropriate information about speech, language and communication.	Describe how information about speech, language and communication is collected where you work.

Strand D / Speech, Language and Communication, and Behavioural, Emotional and Social Development (BESD)

	Competence	Example of indicator of competence
	The practitioner will:	Consider if you can:
Universal D1	You will be aware of the importance of language and communication for behavioural, emotional and social development.	Give an example of how language and communication are important for children and young people's • Behavioural development • Emotional development • Social development.
Universal D2	You will be aware that adults' language and style of communication can affect the behavioural, emotional and social development of children and young people.	Give an example of how adults' language and style of communication affects children and young people's • Behavioural development • Emotional development • Social development.

Strand E / Roles and Responsibilities of Practitioners and how Services are Structured

	Competence	Example of indicator of competence
	The practitioner will:	Consider if you can:
Universal E1	You will be aware of your own roles and responsibilities in your workplace in relation to children and young people's speech, language and communication development. language and communication development.	Describe your own roles and responsibilities in your workplace in relation to children and young people's speech, language and communication development.
Universal E2	You will be aware of the benefits of joint working in supporting speech, language and communication for all children and young people.	Give an example of the benefits of joint working in supporting speech, language and communication for all children and young people.
Universal E3	You will be aware of the different professionals who may be involved in supporting children and young people with particular SLCN.	Give examples of different professionals who may be involved in supporting children and young people with particular SLCN.
Universal E4	You will be able to communicate effectively with other practitioners about the speech, language and communication of the children and young people you work with.	Describe how you communicate effectively with other practitioners about children and young people's speech, language and communication in your workplace.
Universal E5	You will be aware of the main principles of 'Every Child Matters' (ECM)* in relation to children's and young people's speech and language development.	Give an example of how speech, language and communication is relevant to at least one of the ECM outcomes.
Universal E6	You will be aware of any reasonable adjustments for children and young people with SLCN in relation to your workplace's duties under the Disability Discrimination.	Explain where to find relevant information about the Disability Discrimination Act.

Strand F / Special Educational Needs (SEN) in Educational Settings

Not everyone who uses the universal competences of the SLCF will work in educational settings. As a result, some of the competences in strand F may not be directly relevant. However, it may still be useful to be aware of these points.

	Competence	Example of indicator of competence
	The practitioner will:	Consider if you can:
Universal F1	You will be aware that children and young people with SLCN may have special educational needs and may need additional support in educational settings.	Give an example of why a child with SLCN may have SEN. Give an example of the kind of support they may need.
Universal F2	You will be aware of the Government's policy on including children and young people with SEN or SLCN in educational settings.	Identify where to find information on the Government's policy on including children and young people with SEN or SLCN in educational settings.

Strand G / Parents / Carers, Families, Peers and Friends

	Competence	Example of indicator of competence
	The practitioner will:	Consider if you can:
Universal G1	You will be aware of the roles of parents, carers, families, peers and friends in speech, language and communication development.	Describe how different people can influence speech, language and communication development.
Universal G2	You will be aware that there are voluntary-sector and public-sector agencies that provide support for children and young people with SLCN and their families and friends.	Explain where you could find information on other agencies that support children and young people with SLCN, and their families.

Strand H / The Effects of Professional Development in Speech, Language and Communication

	Competence	Example of indicator of competence
	The practitioner will:	Consider if you can:
Universal H1	You will be aware of the benefits of professional development in increasing the positive effect you can have on the speech, language and communication development of all children and young people.	Describe how professional development activities have changed your skills in developing the speech, language and communication skills of the children and young people you work with.

At this level the terms in the Indicators of Competence have the following meanings:

Describe: Provide clear details about a topic or item.
Describe how: Provide clear details about a topic or item, with examples from your own experience and practice where possible.
Explain: Provide clear details about a topic or item, with examples from your own experience and practice where possible.
Identify: Recognise and put in the main points.
List: Write one thing after another.